I LOVE YOU

I LOVE YOU: 65 international poets united against violence against women © 2003 for the authors and artists.
Cover art: "Projected border 1", Anne Longo (USA), copyright © 2002. Used by permission.
c.a.u.s.e. logo by Andrej Troha (Slovenia). Used by permission.
Design and in-house editing by Joe Blades.
Proofreading by Hugh Hazelton and Salvador Torres.
Printed and bound by Sentinel Printing, Yarmouth NS, Canadá.

Printed on Domtar Sandpiper vellum (Lily of the Valley), a 100% non-bleached, non-deinked, post-consumer fibre paper, and Cornwall Coated Cover containing 15% post-consumer fiber.

A version of this book was previously published in a per order-limited, artist edition, individually printed and bound by Gino d'Artali/*c.a.u.s.e.: coalition of artists united for social engagement*.

Ninguna parte de esta publicación puede ser reproducida, almacenada o transmitida en manera alguna ni por ningún medio, sin el previo permiso por escrito del editor o, en el caso de fotocopia u otro medio de reproducción gráfica, sin una licencia del Canadian Copyright Licencing Agency (Access Copyright).

No part of this publication may be reproduced, stored in a retrieval system or transmitted, in any form or by any means, without the prior written permission of the publisher or, in the case of photocopying or other reprographic copying, a licence from the Canadian Copyright Licencing Agency (Access Copyright):

1900-One Yonge St, Toronto ON M5E 1E5. Tel 416 868-1620, 1-800-893-5777, fax 416 868-1621 admin@cancopy.com www.cancopy.com

Broken Jaw Press agradece el apoyo del Consejo de Artes de Canadá y de la Secretaría de Cultura y Deportes de Nuevo Brunswick — División de Desarrollo de las Artes./ Broken Jaw Press gratefully acknowledges the support of the Canada Council for the Arts (for whom this is not an eligible title) and the New Brunswick Culture and Sports Secretariat — Arts Development Branch.

Co-publishers

Broken Jaw Press Inc.
Box 596 Stn A
Fredericton NB E3B 5A6
Canada

www.brokenjaw.com
jblades@brokenjaw.com
tel/fax 506 454-5127

c.a.u.s.e.: *coalition of artists united for social engagement*
Paraguay 1469 Sur
Col. Melchor Ocampo
Ciudad Juárez, Chihuahua, México
www.prophitart.com/facingfaces03
gino@prophitart.com
tel 656 611-80-37

National Library of Canada Cataloguing in Publication Data
I love you : 65 international poets united against violence against women / Gino d'Artali, editor.

Co-published by Coalition of Artists United for Social Engagement.
ISBN 0-921411-31-6

1. Family violence—Poetry. 2. Poetry, Modern—20th century.
I. d'Artali, Gino II. Coalition of Artists United for Social Engagement

PN6101.I34 2003   811'.6080355   C2003-902363-X

I LOVE YOU

65 international poets united against violence against women

Gino d'Artali, Editor

Fredericton • Canadá

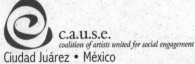
c.a.u.s.e.
coalition of artists united for social engagement
Ciudad Juárez • México

I LOVE YOU
65 international poets united against violence against women

FacingFaces — a tiny message in a bottle thrown into cyberspace 7
  Gino d'Artali, editor

TRIBUTE TO MARÍA LUISA, Gustavo Woijcechowsky, Uruguay . 11
UNTITLED, Alex Lemon, USA 12
SOME SCARS NEVER FADE, Allyn Algar Garavaglia, USA 13
YELLOW ROSE, Anastasia Royal, USA 14
DIECISÉIS, Amit K. Ghosh, India 15
EVAPORATING EARTH, Arcana, The Netherlands 16
SÓLO SON MUJERES, Arminé Ariona, México 17
HYPOCRITE, Avi, México 18
EYESIGHT REVOLUTION, Brad Eubanks, USA 19
DANCING AROUND THE FLAMES, Carlene Parianos, Australia 20
CHILD OF VIOLENCE, Carol Sircoulomb, USA 21
UNKIND, D.C. Bursey, USA 22
THERE WAS NO ONE, Durlabh Singh, Kenya 23
CARTA DE UNA NOCHE APOCALÍPTICA, Erick Falcón,
  México 24
MASKED MAN, Eva Lewarme, Poland 25
TEACH BOYS THAT MEN DO SUCH THINGS, Gene Keller,
  USA 26
JUÁREZ, Gino d'Artali, Belgium 27
A BIRD SANG WHEN I DIED, Hakon Soreide, Norway 28
UNTITLED, Hans-Georg Turstig, Germany 29
FOR THE YOUNG AND DEFENCELESS, Jamie Deramee, USA 30
THE ROPE, Jennifer Beth Burnett, USA 31
SHAME, Jenn Loring, USA 32
FACING FACES, jim "max" christ, USA 33
DESIERTO MANCILLADO, Josse, México 34
NUNCA MÁS, Liz Gonzalez, USA 35
THREE PIECES OF PEACE, Liza Di Georgina, México 39
ORDER OF PROTECTION, Lori Williams, USA 40
WEDDING RING, Lorraine Kelly, UK 42
SRA. KAHLO, Lucina, México 43
DEATH CAME SLOW, Marcia Borell, USA 45
DARK DAYS NIGHT DESCENT, Marques Vickers, USA 47

UNTITLED, Melinda Crider, USA	48
ONE NIGHT, Melisande Luna, USA	49
JUÁREZ, Michaela A. Gabriel, Austria	50
WOUNDED EYES, Michelle Epperson, USA	51
I DON'T KNOW YOUR NAME, Minnetta A. David, USA	52
DICEN QUE LA NIÑA HA VUELTO, Nela Rio, Canada	54
SHADOWS OF THE PAST, Pam Colling, USA	56
PURPLE, Pippa Brush, UK	57
COLLECTIVE GUILT, poeticpiers (I.E.Hogg), UK	58
ICE PICK, Rachelle Wiegand, USA	59
MARÍA GALLARDO, Rafael Melendez, México	62
MIS COSAS FAVORITAS, Robert W. Proctor, USA	65
THROWING CAUTION TO THE WIND, Rose Konda, USA	67
CROSSHAIRS, Sandy Strunk, USA	68
NOTICIA, Selfa A. Chew, México	70
AN EVENING BY THE THAMES, Shanti Weiland, USA	71
CORPSE VISAGE, Sharon Proper, USA	72
THE MACHINE, Shilo Schweizer, USA	73

SIX POETS CONVERSE

ATTENTION DEFICIT, Alice Pero, USA	75
MY FATHER'S FRIEND, MR. HARDY, Mary Hazen-Stearns, USA	76
BEYOND BABI YAR, Ryfkah, USA	77
PULLING A THREAD, Thomas Fortenberry, USA	77
SARAH JANE PASSED THROUGH, Gary Blankenship, USA	81
HONEYSUCKLE NOISE, Marylin Injeyan, USA	83
BATTERED, *starshine*, USA	84
A GOOD WOMAN, Susan Stone Salas, USA	85
THE WOMEN, Tammara Hayimi Slilat, Israel	86
PICNIC, Teemu Lahteenmaki, Finland	87
UNTITLED, TLC Birdsill, USA	88
COTIDIANAS DE MI CIUDAD, Valta Ortega, México	89
EL RÍO MURMURA EL DOLOR DE MARÍA, Verónica Leiton, Chile	90
SI TAN SÓLO ESCUCHARAS … Verónica Olivas, México	91
I LOVE YOU, Windy Sue, USA	93
THE PROMISES, Yéssica, Nicaragua	95

FacingFaces
a tiny message in a bottle thrown into cyberspace

Violence is of all times and all cultures. It is and has always been, unfortunately, part of human nature and probably will be part of human nature as long as we, as a species, exist. Unless, of course, we terminate the problem by terminating ourselves. These last words are obviously spoken by someone who faces violence on a daily basis, and chooses to answer it ironically, to answer it cynically.

Nothing is more true. As the initiator and organizer of *FacingFaces*, I am confronted by violence every single day — not only through the daily headlines in my local newspaper in Ciudad Juárez, Chihuahua, México, but also through simply living here, walking the streets, and looking straight into the "bull's eye".

Now I hear you say, "OK, you're doing your part. So?" Well, I might be doing my part but there is still so much more one can do to create awareness and to say, "No to violence!"

On December 23rd, 2000, I read a headline: "5-year-old girl abducted and severely beaten almost to death by alleged drug dealers".

Reading that article stopped my heart for a minute — or so it felt. It could have been my beloved niece; or the neighboring girl that always smiled to me so sweetly, so trustingly; or my little sister, not that little anymore, but always little in my heart.

And so, from that feeling, I decided to send a clear message in a tiny bottle out into the cyber ocean: "No against violence against women and children." "Call for artists to unite."

Was I expecting an answer? Yes. Was I expecting the response I received? I had hoped for it, but the result of the first exhibition of *FacingFaces 2001* amazed me. We were not all so cynical! Or, at least, I was not the only one who knew that something had to be done to combat violence against women and children.

Eighty-three artists from thirty different countries read that first message, and the result was an exhibition of one hundred and sixty-two diptychs, each one speaking out against violence.

So there I was thinking, "Now I've done my part!"

And, yes, in a certain way I was right. I had done my part. I had brought attention to the case of Janeth, the five-year-old.

But what about this other headline, almost a year later to the day: "Mother of 4 slain by her husband over a divorce dispute".

The same city, but it could have happened in any other city in the world.

Was I done? I didn't think so. So here we were again, a Belgian artist and curator living in Ciudad Juárez, México, a city known for the mass abduction, torture, rape and killings of young women, and this time seventy-six artists and poets from all over the world are saying no to violence against women and children. No to violence in Ciudad Juárez. No to violence anywhere.

On the website, http://www.prophitart.com/facingfaces03, you can visit the gallery of the 2001 project, as well as the poetry and art entries in the 2002 project — touring to El Paso, TX, USA; Fredericton NB, Canada; Los Angeles CA, USA; and the Museo Ex Aduana, Ciudad Juárez, México.

This book, *I Love You: 65 international poets united against violence against women*, is a selection of the poetry entered by poets worldwide to *FacingFaces 2002*.

But why stop here? Have I now done my part? Have we, all the artists and poets involved, done our part?

I don't think so. Why? Because our voices are powerful. You only have to read a few of the poems and feel how they touch your heart, how they change your mind. You only have to visit a few of the artwork pages and feel how your eyes reach the most distant spot in your heart and soul, the part of you that cries out, with us all, "No to violence against women and children!"

Together we can create more awareness, together we can create bigger and bigger waves in our oceans connecting our continents, and together we can say no to violence. I started by saying it would perhaps be best to terminate the human race. I end by saying, instead, let's work together to create a better human race!

Gino d'Artali
Curator, FacingFaces
Director, c.a.u.s.e.: coalition of artists united for social engagement

I dedicate this collection of poetry to María Luisa Carsoli Berumen, victim of a brutal murder, to all women and children who are victims of domestic and/or sexual violence, and to my mother who was a victim for the most part of her life, but who never stopped believing in me.

— Gino d'Artali

TRIBUTE TO MARÍA LUISA

qué cara la caricia cruel
qué descarado el desquicio
tu cara quebrada

qué desprecio que precio tan caro
tu pelo maría luisa, tu pelo suelto
qué descontrol querer controlar
qué no querer
qué tantísimo no querer
ni siquiera a sí mismo ni si

disolver el amor
liquidarlo de rojo líquido
disolverlo
verlo disociado

disuelto el amor
el pelo se suelta: un golpe

pájara su pelo al aire ríe el pelo
sujeto del movimiento
tu pelo
tu pelo maría luisa, tu pelo revuelto

la mano del corazón del puñal
no puede ni siquiera tocarte atarte cortarte

tu pelo maría luisa, tu pelo muerto

Gustavo Woijcechowsky

UNTITLED

Beneath burnt-out streetlights
Angels collect pain like trash.
Blanketed in night's solitude they try
to swallow the entire world's sorrow.
Hands broken, tattooed with the symmetry
of weathered scars, they work tirelessly.
We will have our heaven too,
they whisper and everywhere
Storms are brewing. Window-perched
Above a cluster of sunflowers,
a jar teeming with nails rattles,
Power lines quiver uncontrollably.
Rain explodes and the earth is filled
with this hope, this coarse music.

Alex Lemon

SOME SCARS NEVER FADE

Within unseen walls a silenced spirit walks
to haunt the living with truth
with the memories of her life —
and the dreams left betrayed.
In whispers which chill the flesh
in screams which shudder the soul
in cries that stir the heart
She moves in the silence of a photograph
which haunt not from without — but within.
From the shadows to the Light
Her image a tapestry of fear
Of the dark legends yet untold
Still sealed in a box of pain
With no voice and no name ...
And it is up to the living to open the box.

Allyn Algar Garavaglia

YELLOW ROSE

Even dried and dead,
a yellow rose is enough
a yellow handkerchief is the last
they saw of her
if they could be sure
she was gone for good.
She would never do that to them.
Her children, her dark, bearded husband
stood in the too yellow sun
and watched it waving
goodbye or surrender
or freedom in
the last breath of breeze
torn on the rosebush
she tended, fluttering
her name is, was
Rosa, and on her empty
coffin yellow roses sleep.
Her littlest, Martita, asked
for red ones, or, at the very least,
bright pink, but Rosa's words
came softly as petals,
"Yellow is for caution cuidado,
and I want to live a long life."

Anastasia Royal

DIECISÉIS

I came to in a gutter,
feel the pain of my hips barely moving,
vergüenza between my legs.
La policca me dice, "What happened, chica?"
He's an older man, very official;
His moustache shone in the distant light.
_-*_-*_-*_-*_-*_-
I was on Avenida Dieciséis,
Waking really
from a crowded dream.
The cars rushed towards el Puente
or home for the madrugada.
The bars had closed
Vértigo, Ajúa ... todos.
I was walking a mi casa — sola
No tenía dinero para el taxi
No tenía amigos en mi vida
Mi novio se fue
with someone else.
With friends, he said. Amables.
¡Mentiroso! Todos estàn borrachos, or
With that pinche cabrona
with long black hair,
who was winking at him, at
his big, gold chain as
he held me coldly while
slurping his michelada.
A las dos in the morning
La hora de los sueños
Sweet dreams of togetherness
con mi amorcito ...
I was walking alone on Dieciséis
As a short, dark man
threw me into the gutter.
Why?

Amit K. Ghosh

EVAPORATING EARTH

At last at last
floating minds,
who is that speaking,
fairytales
Vision
surrender understanding
the enduring mind

Without time floating
impregnate
the first blossom
from the almond tree.

Mountain frost gliding
through your morning valley,
a bird picking seeds
from other times.
Give birth to new fruit,
high and far
flying her paws
there evaporating earth

    Arcana

SÓLO SON MUJERES

En esta frontera
el decir mujeres
equivale a muerte
enigma y silencio.
Seres desechables
que desaparecen
cruelmente apagados
por manos cobardes.
Y todos nos vamos
volviendo asesinos
con la indiferencia
con el triste modo
en que las juzgamos:
"gente de tercera"
"carne de desierto"
sólo son mujeres
una nota roja
viento pasajero
que a nadie le importa.

Arminé Ariona

HYPOCRITE

March's sun
vertically falls at noon,
I lean over the burning sand from the sun,
burning sun that drifts between my fingers,
sand that smells like fear,
sand that smells like horror,
sand that smells like pity.
Savage hands raping emotions,
burning is the blood that drifts between evil fingers,
sand that smells like pain,
sand that smells like shame.
The wind suffocates the heat,
wind that witnesses abuse,
wind that erases all tracks,
wind that plays with the sand
making waves of peace…
Hypocrite border…
Hypocrite by showing your face of peace.

Avi

EYESIGHT REVOLUTION
For The Young And Defenceless

you hold your breath and wonder
if it isn't fate that all your tiny defections
thrive on an almond-hard fist
rummaging in Papa's coat pocket for his cigarettes
as you count the many hours he spends delivering you good intentions
a quiet man who eats pork
for Papa you keep your buttons green
smiling when the sirens fail to sound
your nodes separated to absorb greater impact
until nearing fatal vertigo
you discover that the moth travelling half a mile an hour
isn't your brother
but that one day we may all begin to look like that.

Brad Eubanks

DANCING AROUND THE FLAMES

He returns from the land of the gods
white petals shower the paved courtyard
bass thumps through closed doors
wispy smoke trails around freshly
washed clothes
Nerves once sleeping stand at attention,
Keys and pin codes, lock it all up,
yes, scum, yes, fuck me, yes, selfish bitch
its only a vase, a new plaster wall
A six-foot raging inferno,
sixteen, going on two
Sweep up the glass and rest before he wakes ...

Carlene Parianos

CHILD OF VIOLENCE

She was locked up in the closet
at the age of eight
by her mother the awful woman
She was locked up in her bedroom frequently with him
his machete at her throat
as he invaded her small body
She danced and smiled
danced some more
in small confines the awful woman watching
She kicked the door in
screaming her rage
at her mother the awful woman
She was dragged by her hair
in the vortex of the tornado
twisted arms head banged till she bled
by the awful woman
She dances now in the fetal position
of the closet
the awful woman smiling

Carol Sircoulomb

UNKIND

Ice water veins keep you calm cool and collected
So you can strike the warm loving unsuspected
You are a surgeon the like not seen before or again
You can slice out a heart and not break the skin
Here I am sitting at the table
Ghosts of laughter are able
To comfort and torment
All that they find
You left my mind
Unkind
To me

D.C. Bursey

THERE WAS NO ONE

There was no one
Only the sound of my footsteps
Or perhaps the sound of my breath
Disturbing some wandering brief
A tone wedged in whispering grief.

There was no one, only a shadow
Walking on the incumbent street
Memories of pathways going stray
With hands held in an evening greet.

Perhaps only in footsteps of the lost
In dances of the rains of whirling trot
Murmurs of north in dirges of drain
Hungers of the earth in cities of pain.

Durlabh Singh

CARTA DE UNA NOCHE APOCALÍPTICA
(letanía de una madre asesinada)

Hoy amanece mientras todos nos volvemos eternos
Y ciegos ...
[latido ... latido ... latido]
Veo lágrimas derramándose por las mejillas de la inconsciencia
Veo fuego del otro lado del espejo ...
[latido ... latido ... coraje]
Brisas melancólicas monitorean el tibio aire
Y la lluvia cae ...
[latido ... latido ... pausa]
La lúgubre tarde cubre el suspiro del sol juarense
Los juguetes quietos quietos ...
[latido ... latido ... llanto]
No es lo mismo la avena fría
Ni darle de comer al perro ...
[latido ... latido ... suspiro]
Vamos tarde de vuelta a nuestra tierra
Mamá se quedó aquí ...
[latido ... latido ... silencio]
in memoriam

Erick Falcón

MASKED MAN

I am tired of endless drones,
busy blues, filling out blank time.
I am tired of waiting as the wheel of fortune spins,
praying the needle will land on pink again.
I am fed up with whining, crying, fighting, wasting time.
Also, with endless promises of rosy endings
by voiceless people of various cults.
I am tired of snoopy, droopy spectators,
sniffing at secrets yet unborn.
At those who herald good news views,
one day and the next,
prophesize doom and gloom.
I am sick of eating, digesting
and eliminating the same stale,
recycled food and air.
I am ready for the kiss of eternal bliss,
after years of suffering and scorn.
Masked Man — leave me alone,
let me soar to regions yet unknown,
alone and whole.

Eva Lewarme

TEACH BOYS THAT MEN DO SUCH THINGS

count the bodies, count the bruises, hairs, limbs
numbers of numbers equal to nothing

dirt in a mouth, pebbles over eyes, each hair crawling away
scream-echoes in the desert night shiver the stars

10,000 children, 10,000 sisters, 10,000 mothers
their blood a rust on the sands of the desert

in the dark city, a man with darkness stalks
a shadow with a face of light - his eyes, his money

or a gang of wild boys, keepers of chaos
lost in their dark fantasy, locked in that reality

prayers for those women, cries for revenge, justice
poems about violence written in blood

since woman first took root in a garden
the lessons were always for the sons

if the boy knows the slap, he calluses
if he learns the caress, he flourishes

teach boys that men do such things
teach boys to sing and dance under the moon

Gene Keller

JUÁREZ

Juárez,
where surrealism rules
or so one says,
pointing out signs
on rock and bark.

Where I only see
bloodstains
of another young life
smashed.

Yes I do
visit the ladies bars
and wonder
whom will she marry first:
the narco or the politician?
What difference is there anyway
Both selling opium to the people.

Yes I do
buy chiclets from children lost
and wonder if ever they'll help
to chase the bitter taste on my lips
in fear of finding them
dead on the street.
Juárez,
where I live
and dream,
or at least
try to fulfil my dreams,
however too often haunted
by the indescribable

Surrealism?
Escapism?

¡Quién sabe!
Me vale madre

    Gino d'Artali

A BIRD SANG WHEN I DIED

I heard a bird sing when I died,
And if this eternal sleep
But one memory preserves in dreams
That through the darkness shine,
The bird singing when I died
Would be the memory of mine.

Hakon Soreide

UNTITLED

Terror stricken
Fearful eyes
Running for shelter and life.
Whom can I trust if I must?
And I see and I flee
And I am not free
And I certainly have no choice.

At least the deceased
are at peace — are at PEACE?

Hans-Georg Turstig

FOR THE YOUNG AND DEFENCELESS

you hold your breath and wonder
if it isn't fate that all your tiny defections
thrive on an almond-hard fist
rummaging in Papa's coat pocket for his cigarettes
as you count the many hours he spends delivering you good intentions
a quiet man who eats pork
for Papa you keep your buttons green
smiling when the sirens fail to sound
your nodes separated to absorb greater impact
until nearing fatal vertigo
you discover that the moth travelling half a mile an hour
isn't your brother
but that one day we may all begin to look like that.

Jamie Deramee

THE ROPE

Because of your touch my life is forever changed.
My entire self-image has been rearranged.
Your hands should have protected, Instead they projected,
Nightmares and bad memories. I am forever affected.
Your lips should have whispered loving words set in soft tones.
Instead they only pushed through vile sounds, breathless moans.
Your skin should have smelled of Irish Spring and cologne
Instead my mind is implanted with the stench of foul sweat and hormones.
I should have been playing with my childhood friends.
Instead of satisfying the fetishes of a much older man.
Your life was shattered that day my voice rose.
I may have tightened the noose, but you strung the rope.
Every strand woven by your heavy hands.
The knot tied more tightly with every sickening demand.
I hope your breath leaves you much slower than my innocence did.
May you feel the same suffocation that I did as a kid.
When you get to hell may you be stripped of your soul.
The way you stripped me of mine at only 8 years old.
I think, what a coward, as you swing to and fro.
Mouth hung wide open, feet dragging the floor.
Hanging from the noose of the rope that you wove.

Jennifer Beth Burnett

SHAME

I am the child without a mother
I am the mother without a daughter.
I am the fear that holds me captive
and as sure is my silence
until I am the body lying cold in a grave.
I am the faces flashed on the evening news.
Missing murdered.
I am a family's grief and a husband's shame.
I am the cry for help in tear-swollen eyes.
I am the one it was too late to save.
I am the memory of a battered body
and a shattered soul.
I am the voice of your sister
your mother
your daughter
your friend
And I am you.

Jenn Loring

FACING FACES

ciudad sin luz,
1-22-01 marked you
when narcotraficantes
scarred another daughter.

her muffled screams
went unnoticed
tumbling from speeding car
and childhood.

times of unconcern and apathy
are torn from every face, from every thought,
from now on.

juárezes of the world,
your janeths cry out;
terror looks from pleading windows.
blindness makes it so.

averted faces and eyes strangle
as surely as guilty hands,
the light and innocence of our young
until faces turn from shadows.

    jim "max" christ

DESIERTO MANCILLADO
en memoria de Liliana Alejandra

17 años y está muerta
mujer, trabajadora, madre,
no quisiera creerlo, pero es cierto
misoginia y barbarie desatada
estadística y realidad
las mujeres del desierto
gritan dolor y rebeldía, hasta ahogar la garganta
en un puñado de dolor arena, dolor de sol,
dolor de sangre,
visión que duelo de terror amenazante,
/ ni una más /
gritan las mujeres del desierto,
del Valle,
de la Sierra de Guadalupe,
de Lomas de Poleo,
de Palo Chino, de Anapra.
/ Ni una más /
gritan las mujeres del desierto,
ni una más ...
/ Ni una más .../

Josse

NUNCA MÁS

    I
In Ciudad Juárez,
in an open lot
a field hand
cutting down grass
stumbled over a young
woman's body
He thought he had tripped
onto a dumped bag of junk
when he heard
the flies buzzing
She lay face-up,
expressionless, naked
except for socks, her hands
bound with shoe laces
Close by, police found
two more bodies and five
female skeletons
Cuerpo uno, tres, ocho

    II
Claudia Gonzales' mother
only recognized her daughter by
the ponytail and blouse
left on her bones
Months after
investigators shut down
their inspection of the lot,
two boys found a clump
of hair, women's shoes,
ripped panties, and
Claudia's overalls
Her mother hugs them tight
as though Claudia lives inside

III

Cuerpo nueve, cuerpo
cincuenta, cuerpo cien,
cuerpo doscientos,
cuerpo, cuerpo, cuerpo
Black numbered
pink wooden stakes testify
Since 1993, more than 300
girls and women
have turned up
with cracked skulls,
snapped necks, raped,
decomposed, shot, stabbed,
strangled. And sometimes
just bones
All thrown out
like used fast food wrappers

IV

When another broken body
is found,
production doesn't halt
at the maquiladoras
Everyday, more girls
and women arrive,
fill the empty spaces
on assembly lines
Más y más, más y más
More who can't afford to
turn down a job paying
a dollar an hour. More
who have to walk
across the desert alone

V

In a city where men don't go to jail
for beating and raping
their girlfriends and wives,
murderers can be choosy.
This one (or these guys) mangled 80-90, so far
He takes factory workers
and school girls.
He chops their hair off,
carves their skin, slashes
their breasts. He likes slim
teen-aged girls with long dark hair
like Irma Monreal's only daughter
who was saving for her quinceañera
but didn't make it home
before her fifteenth birthday
Instead of waltzing with her girl
on the dance floor, dust devils
swirl by as she prays
at Esmeralda's grave site

VI

Mujeres conocidas muertas
Loved women murdered
Too many pink crosses
More than 300
Nine years
One city
Officials offered prophecies
live on TV. A few blamed the dead
saying they wandered streets
dressed too revealingly
Presidente Fox made
promises
Suspects were arrested,
tortured to confess
The police announced
the cases solved
But the females
are still slaughtered

VII

These women are mis
hermanas. Our veins
cross the border
like Bridge of the Americas.
Am I naive to believe that
if they were born on this side,
if the killings happened here,
the count
could never get so high —
no matter that they're
brown and poor?
How many more families
have to tape photos
of their missing daughters
on storefront windows?
How many more crosses
planted in the desert dirt
¿Cuántos más cuerpos?
How many more
screams ignored
until the mass murder
is stopped? ¿Cuántos?

Liz Gonzalez

THREE PIECES OF PEACE

Sell me three pieces of your peace,
come back crossing my path,
you must know that the night at the border is darker than others,
and the crosses from the past are forgotten too soon,
lend me the snail of your ear,
may it walk slowly on the tracks of silence,
through the labyrinths of the souls that try to return home still,
without knowing that they have already died,
and inside of an adobe room only salty diamonds illuminate the darkness
of the mothers that suddenly were left dry and dusty, old statues,
while the ashes of 400 lost girls dilute
day by day over the anonymous asphalt,
between indifferent breaths,
and you ...
Meanwhile you,
sell me three pieces of your peace,
for here, nothing happens.

Liza Di Georgina

ORDER OF PROTECTION

It could be typed by a child:
ORDER OF PROTECTION

flimsy piece of paper meant to be
a shield
a barrier
a defence.

Oh yes, Mr. Lawmaker, of course it works!
Just ask the lady with her brains blown out
all over the used car she was just about to sell;
hers was neatly tucked into her purse,
as safe and sound as she thought it made her.
Her husband pulled the trigger, and
there was not a drop of blood on her
ORDER OF PROTECTION!

Just ask the girl who was chopped up
and buried all over her suburban neighborhood;
hers was in the pocket of her Calvin's. Had she time
to pull it out, I'm sure her boyfriend would have taken flight,
his axe and insanity held off yet again … After all, it is an
ORDER OF PROTECTION!

Just ask the woman who has moved a dozen times,
uprooting her kids, losing jobs, going broke,
simply to escape the wrath of a man enamoured of her;
hers was lost in move 5, perhaps 6. She was
too busy running to notice.
And she is still too busy running to stop for a new
ORDER OF PROTECTION!

Just ask me. Mine is right here by my side;
next to my gun.
Just in case the law doesn't work …
again.

BANG
Oh yes, Mr. Lawmaker ...
BANG!!!!

Lori Williams

WEDDING RING

I can't move my arm today
You stupid bitch
And my vision is a little blurred
You stupid bitch
It's hot and sunny outside
But I'll stay indoors
Can't you do anything right?
And I'll make dinner perfect tonight
And lay the table exactly
Nothing out of place
You ugly cunt, ugly and stupid
It hurts to walk
But I won't limp or stumble
You're a fucking mess
Knocking at the door
She asks me to leave him
You're nothing without me
She asks me to go with her
She doesn't understand
I'll kill your whole pathetic family
I have to go shower
Have to get clean

I remember

With this ring I thee wed
With this ring I control

    Lorraine Kelly

SRA. KAHLO

Frida, dónde estás mujer ...
Where are you?
You died for our sins,
promising us the resurrection,
a rebirth
our self-worth intact.

We had only to bury you,
release you
and that monkey
on your back.

You jangled and giggled
a beautiful, moist jewel ...
twenty silver bangles
singing
from each wrist.

Your blinding white camellias
sitting like a crown,
your hibiscus red-orange lips
calling us forth to watch
you sweep your men,
your pain,
into a pile
there — in the centre
of your world.

And you laughed, Frida,
knowing to do so
would hurt.
You gathered your breath, Frida,
knowing to do so
would hurt.
You exhaled loudly
a breath of raw perfume

A fire that stained
a hundred canvas flags
and sent your name
flying
across the ages ... a mad Mexican dove
who seeks
only to soothe women
who hurt.

Women who hurt.

    Lucina

DEATH CAME SLOW

death came slow
a final release
from pain
from disbelief

how did this happen
what did I do
why
no rescue
except in death's
embrace

where is my
mother
where is my
brother

alone
I
rest
with my murdered
sisters

body exposed
empty eyes gaze
toward home
empty

bones
picked clean
some broken
blue purple
skin
rots away

help
help me
please stop
help me please

find me
bring me home
save my
living
sisters

Marcia Borell

DARK DAYS NIGHT DESCENT

enter the dense night bravely
beauty
as a darkness descends on another day
lacking the lightness of youth
innocence separated
engulfed into the depths
of rest eternal

Marques Vickers

UNTITLED

I heard the coyotes
yapping
but no one
answered us.

Melinda Crider

ONE NIGHT

Hard-bitten night,
a black of the mind fantasy —
cum East of San Francisco reality,
beat a new blueprint of me.

In the gloom of pylons I was
a dove under the Dunbarton Bridge;
where men ran fire opals
down my thighs.

I became their fluid hours
measured in thrusts and bangs.
Clocks rang, and I flew,

free, across bay salt flats,
at last, as mud thick with clams
sucked off my shoes.

Joy, in the burn of a cigarette,
washed bloodslick and come from a mouth
split wide in redemption.

Melisande Luna

JUÁREZ

Dry country surrounds you,
a desert from which fear creeps
every night, through cracks in favela walls,
into women's hearts.

It comes with the wind panting
a hundred names: María, Teresa, Janeth,
the names of those who cried tears
the colour of blood,
whose bones splintered in the hands
of men, self-righteous and cruel.
Juárez, your wells run dry,
your colourful gardens wilt.

In this place, even children's laughter
has ceased to be innocent.

Michaela A. Gabriel

WOUNDED EYES

Eyes that pierce to your
very soul and ask
why did I go to bed hungry
why did you not protect me
why did you abuse me
in my little fragile
heart and soul

Eyes that ask
who will make my world
a place where I
can be safe
and who will
make these eyes fill with joy
instead of fear and
terror and tears
Tiny eyes that show strength
even when times
are cruel and mean and tough
and little eyes
that ask what did I do
to make you abandon me
when i needed you

These are the eyes
that will haunt us
and leave us ashamed
if we do not advocate
for those who are
too small to demand
justice and peace

Michelle Epperson

I DON'T KNOW YOUR NAME

I cried last night
The first time about this moment
A moment in time you took from me
No, not took ... you ripped from me
I pay the price for your actions
I live with the results of your previous choices
I didn't ask to ever see your face
Yet in the night did you come to me
Ripped me away
Hid me in a dark dank place
Brutalized and tore away what little I had rebuilt
I don't know your name

Forever you will be that dark face, mean and hideous
The hours are enough to torment me for years to come
Yet you may have left a demon
A horrid fatal demon in your wake
I cried last night
I don't know your name
Life was looking up
Going forward, new beginnings
Un-sinking that sunken ship
Yes that is what I was doing
Working so hard
Now ... I face YOUR vile demon
I don't know what the answer is
Right now it is just a torment
A battering in the mind
Hopes and dreams put on hold
How terribly unfair that you
Can play around in my head
I don't know your name

I cried and grieved and let loose some of my anger
I am angry and wounded
You may have signed my death sentence

All for what? Why? To what purpose were your actions?
Why did you choose me to violate?
Why stumble upon my path?
Your demon, that may become my own
And then I would have to live with you, every day

I don't even know your name!

Minnetta A. David

DICEN QUE LA NIÑA HA VUELTO

tarde de luna temprana
    calles llenas de gente
    callejones de penumbra
la niña camina sola

ojos turbios la persiguen
    oculta la cara fea
    ¡la niña camina sola
con ojos que la persiguen!

la escuela ya está muy lejos
    la casa se acerca lenta
    los ojos ya tienen manos
la niña camina sola

paredes que se entrechocan
    parecen garganta oscura
    los pasos ya se apresuran
la niña camina sola
salto de olas furiosas
    estruendo de sofocado terror
    las manos buscan la carne
de la niña que andaba sola

aliento de fragua quemada
    endurecido pene de fuego
    busca atrevido las piernas
la niña sola en el suelo

busca desgarra atraviesa
    agudo dolor de espadas
    corta a la niña vencida
la niña vejada sola

    * * *

Hace rato que la luna
   ya puebla la noche entera.
   La gente busca a la niña
entre sollozos de pena.

¡Las madres trenzan sus manos
   para proteger a sus hijas
   los padres sofocan gemidos
que cortan más que cuchillos!

La gente ahogándose grita
   ¡aquí la niña que viene
   trayendo la falda blanca
cubierta de sangre negra!

La gente llora diciendo
   la niña tiene lágrimas secas
   en las azules mejillas
abiertas en huesos rotos.

¡Dicen que la niña corre
   silencio enredado en el pelo
   abiertos ojos perdidos
que cubren manos llenas de gritos!

y la niña que viene mira
   enloquecida de asombro
   semen y sangre corriendo
entre sus piernas heridas.

¡Aquí la niña que viene!
¡Basta ya!

   Nela Rio

SHADOWS OF THE PAST

Daily I walk down the long corridors.
Head and shoulders down, I trod lonely halls.
But today a chance movement caught my eye,
Dimly I saw shadows along the walls.
I looked once again and the shadows moved.
As I stared closely they came into focus.
The spectres of children who are long dead.
Their haunted eyes watching as we pass by.
Today's trial will draw no crowds to watch.
The victim was only an unknown child.
No media frenzy to draw a crowd.
For no rich man's darling was this little one.
Today the "victims" press into the court.
They fill the benches and stand in the aisles,
And only I have noticed their presence,
As they wait and pray for some small justice.
To most they are but shadows of the past.
No one wept tears when they too were murdered,
But I watch as they silently gather,
Their haunted eyes filled with tears and sorrow.

Pam Colling

PURPLE

Still while our beautiful boy
swam in the dark red of my belly,
you marked my breasts purple yellow

Stroked corn-silk hair of our babies,
then dragged me from the belly of sleep
with your fist and
the palm of your hand

Pushing against hate and shame,
beating an elaborate tattoo on flesh and bone,
skin blooming into flowers
of knowledge and silence

You did not even ask my forgiveness
but waited instead for the
redemption of morning

Pippa Brush

COLLECTIVE GUILT

Bruised and battered, bleeding,
who counts up the cost?
Of the many women.
in the legions of the lost.

Seduced, abused and murdered
abandoned then at will.
How can society tolerate
these macho brutes who kill?

Where are the protectors,
guardians of the law?
Are women so inferior,
they're not worth caring for?

It does not seem to matter,
to the powers that be.
That such suffering is widespread.
Who cares, now the bitch is dead?

Next one may be your daughter,
your sister or your wife.
Isn't it time we made a stand
to protect every woman's life,

We can't change human nature,
there is no reason why.
Civilized societies.
Should not make a try.

poeticpiers (I.E.Hogg)

ICE PICK

It is as if he can sense
my vulnerabilities.
Smell them, even.

Deer caught
in the headlights,
nowhere to run,
to hide
from the ghost
of childhood past.
It has come
to claim me.

I had asked
the magic questions
only hours ago,
while speaking with my Father.
"How can you forgive someone
that has never
said that they were sorry?
Never owned up
to the heartbreak
that they inflicted?
The precious trust
that they destroyed?"

"Don't be surprised," he had said.

Five hours later,
alone, scared and off guard,
The ringing phone
breaks the brick silence
like an ice pick
hitting the block.
This time,
it is him.

Fifteen years.
He waited
fifteen damned years
to call me and apologize.
Suddenly so sorry
that he robbed me
of my innocence.

Could he truly be sorry
that I had suffered
because he couldn't
keep his hands off of
little girls?

His words hung in my air
for hours.
"You were my world,
you, of all people,
I never meant to hurt you,
I mean YOU," he said.

I tell myself
that this
is only another thing,
just another thing
to get through.

But in truth,
this is THE
thing
to get through.

I look up,
see the reflection
in the cobalt
gazing ball.

A broken little girl,
curled up
in anger and anguish.

I look down
at my knuckles,
crimson red
from the heartache
balled tightly in my fist.

    Rachelle Wiegand

MARÍA GALLARDO

Naranja dulce limón partido,
María yo te conocía,
oh yes I knew you.

I knew you when — when you and I
used to go to different schools together.

Yes ... yo te conocía — María.

I knew you when — when my suenos
were the color of a salsa picante
And castañetas clicked in my head
like crickets dressed like mariachis
in hot summer nights.

Yo te conocía — María

I knew you María — when el cucuyo,
el mentado chamuco hid
underneath my bed and scratched the
floor with his diablo fingernails.
and you protected me while I hid
underneath the blankets — las cobijas
and ate pinole like
a holy Eucharist one last time.

Yo te conocía — María,

Oh yes I knew you
when you laid with the gachupín —
the false feathered serpent — Cortés
and freed me from
the oppression of Tonatiuh and Tezcatlipoca
gods of worlds I never knew

Yo te conocía — María.

When you freed me forever
from the altars that held my beating corazón
as I waited for a resurrection that never came.
And I condemned you Malinche?

I knew you María — yo te conocía.

When el mundo was coming to an end
with the rain fire of Quiauntonatium
y la noche ... the night escurriría
you stood ready with your doble cananas.
Your bandoliers and your woman's scorn.
You and Adelita — and beat a chingadazos
El gachupín's butt — his culo.

Yo te conocía María ... I knew you when.

When you waited at the kitchen table
en la cocina for me to return,
from barrio wars that were not mine
in prayer — "La Bamba" blaring
through the night and I came home
loco por la mota y el caballo
the elixir of my oppressive Aztec Gods

Yo te conocía ... María

I knew you María and watched you
when you shackled yourself to the hot cocina
stove la estufa and made tortillas de amor
that I ate with mantequilla.
And you wore that same old apron,
stained with the past memorias
of meals prepared with love for me.

Yo te conocía ...

I knew you when María — And even
when the sun promised never to return.
Still you said to me, close your eyes,
and you filled them with pan dulce.
And you hugged me singing,
Naranja dulce limón partido
dame un abrazo que yo te pido.

I knew you María Gallardo. Yo te conocía.

And I never thanked you, gave you las gracias
But las palabras failed me. Pero siempre yo fui
muy pendejo — mea culpa.

Rafael Melendez

MIS COSAS FAVORITAS

another perspective

Prologue:

Goodness has a thousand faces,
Malevolence, some believe,
has a thousand more.
And many of them
mock us south of the border.

Look at this face.
It is one of them.
Look hard. Be not cowed.
It will stare at you one day
unless you deal with it, now.

———————

When she begged for mercy,
that was a favorite thing.
But I wanted more, you see.
I wished her groveling at my feet
the fear of me — and my knife — complete.
That pleased me, another favourite thing.

I do this on dusty, trash-strewn flats
South of the city, no one around
to hear her screams, to stop me, Whack!
From knocking her down.
That was heaven, another favourite thing.

My power was absolute,
me, a sly nobody
sure got someone's attention, as would any brute
that day, and the next, and the next.
I plucked these other bodies
from street corners
with offers of free rides.

I exploited them, sure.
Many were glad to save a bus or taxi buck,
And I was there with a lure
to hell in a culvert's dry muck.
Almost my favourite of favourite things.

Why almost? The best thing was
no one else cared.
Politicians, cops, employers ...
They had priorities, their own favourite things.
And these chicks were everywhere. I got "freebies," frankly speaking,
Because nobody but ME cared.

That was my most favourite thing.

Robert W. Proctor

THROWING CAUTION TO THE WIND

Yellow is for caution
the dead dried rose on your empty coffin said
or, rather — meant.

Your yellow handkerchief with the rainbow embroidered
edge is dirty now.   Forever left behind.
Husband, children, family, will not wash
this memory of you.
It's all they have   the last hold
you held onto

before you and over 300 women in
Cuidad Juárez disappeared into
a fury of serial sexual femicide.

Red is for life
the vibrant red rose held by your daughter said
or, rather — meant.

Women all over the world gather rose petals
for your little daughter, Martita.
Wild rose petals — pink, yellow and red.
We make perfumed, soft water and
scent our handkerchiefs, let them blow in the wind.

Our square coloured cloths carry a message
to those who consumed and disposed of
you, Rosa, and the other women:

Yellow, caution. All blood dries red.

    Rose Konda

CROSSHAIRS

Targets of beautiful towering grace
Prey of the malformed minds
In the perilous mutations of species

Women are your children
They are your Mothers
They are your Sisters
And your Lovers

Annihilation stalks
Left to defend themselves
Alone, while they bury their dead

The horror in Ciudad Juárez
Tries to summon the paid protectors
But the incantation is mute

From the primitive throat
Would be torn the last call of defense
Had the protectors terminated the threats

Were humans one with the wild
They'd not be defiled
For the pack would eliminate the insurgents

Where are the warriors
With honor so vast
When will they answer the broken cries?

The assassin has no skill
Needs no scope to target kill
Because the protectors' silence
Has sanctioned their intent

Abomination
Assassination
Civilization
Extermination

Who gave you consent
To devalue their lives?
Scavenge your own

Although the fear hangs in the wind
While the predators nap
And replenish their cruel desires

These women now maintain the pack
And they will rise and growl
You have forfeited your rights

Sandy Strunk

NOTICIA

Te veo en el fondo de una hoja
escondida tu mirada entre el murmullo
de los sordos que no vieron tu garganta
apagándose en un monte de basura.
Operadora / consorte de una línea
que rasga esta ciudad en cuatro partes.
Si las manos se ocupan de engranajes,
quién cargará tu ataúd sobre el presagio
de otras niñas y otras manos en sepulcros,
colinas de la arena hecha silencio.
Tu frente desnuda se teje entre las pruebas,
de que el crimen fue tuyo, de tu ropa,
del horario asignado por los jueces
y de un cuchillo entre el trabajo y tus tres hijos.
Cierro el periódico, mi inocencia comprobada,
llego puntual al concierto de asesinos.

Selfa A. Chew

AN EVENING BY THE THAMES

I don't need to smack that grin off.
Your hand's down your pants again,
slutting through the city,
reaching for my skin.
Hand's working your crotch and
the river's cool and oiled.
You leer over the railing.
It's evening, and you're done
at the office, Italian suit
all oiled and sticking to skin.
You sniff my legs, imagine me nude
pointed, prickled, heel flat
sticking to your crotch
as if *I* glued it there myself.
Pricked, your pants pointed
in flesh thinking
my hips, *my* breasts, *my* skin
glued to bones have lured
your hands to bulge
and have made your flesh unpretty,
boned and bound. You are
stuck and grinning, and I am free
and pretty used to your kind,
slinking through the city — *slut*.

Shanti Weiland

CORPSE VISAGE

A restless spirit needing more
A gaze upon thine countenance
As thy tears   thy pale palette of eclectic storm-soaked coloirs
drape translucent skin with mottled hues
mixing creating this corpse visage returning your stare ...
with every bittersweet smile
stinging blows rain down like the apologies
ghostly in appearance
fading smoke
lingering stench
vile temptation
those hands
that bring such love ...
wander amongst thy gravestones
lost dreams
fragments of illumination
spirit broken
back bent to the task of raising thy man-child
for that is what belief is all about ...
light thy candles anew
from behind clouded
blind eyes
let them gleam upon reality
beg of them to dye away mottled blotches
to Polariod for posterity who thine are
and what thine are truely worth
for only then shall thy be free of chains
free of abuse
free of his brand of love
to find clarity
to find sight
to see beyond this corpse visage.

Sharon Proper

THE MACHINE

It all feeds you know.
What you're trying to use up in me,
It drives you farther from your purpose.
You bloody me trying to lighten yourself.
Strengthen yourself.
Only to fall deeper into the cogs that push me higher.
You take your fists,
Your knives, Your words,
Dig them into me.
You drain into me all that you want,
Need,
To not feel incomplete.
Your control is mine,
Every time you look in my eyes.
Eyes on my body.
Body on your mind.
Mind in your hands.
You lose Ability.
You lose your Self.
And break it into me.
You want the rights of gods
To puppeteer me.
Her.
Us.
Anyone.
Everyone.
You have no divine rights.
I do not belong to you.
I will not.
I come through this.
Every time.
Conquer you and all that you've done to me.
You bring me closer to you own catharsis.
Each time you empty your frustration,
Take a little more freedom from me.
I gain more.

I am light.
I am heaven-touched and spinning a new life.

Shilo Schweizer

ATTENTION DEFICIT

"The kid's impossible. He runs all around the room. There's nothing we can do with him." — Teacher of 3rd grade student

In the morning, it's TV and toothpaste,
colourful cereal, red white and blue, FDA sugar and chemical mix
Cartoons before breakfast, Mommy's aspirin, Daddy's booze,
Actors whining on the soap opera after the news
Man abuse, woman abuse, carefully scripted,
edgy voices to fill spaces between Mommy's moods
Child immune to jitters on the tube, runs in circles, pretends he's not here
does what Daddy does, copies TV actor's sneer
Child has attention-deficit, it's true
No one notices while he fiddles with his shoes
Mom brought him to the doctor on teacher's advice
Ritalin will fix him, it's not easy, it will have to do
Doc smiles blandly and shows them the door after minutes of talk,
insurance will cover it, just fill the papers and walk
No one sees the drug will make him an addict
Whose attention deficit is this?
Now he's in the classroom, he must sit and stand
Pledge of Allegiance, words misunderstood he must chant on demand
What is "indivisible"? No one bothers to explain
Should he be invisible? a republic? justice?
He's zoning out, no one sees him or cares,
he's already labeled ADD, so why expect him to understand?
There's one thing that's sure, he won't miss his medication
He needs pills to be here, to sit quiet and be still
He will get his prescription filled and refilled
He's got his whole life before him, does anyone know
what will happen when he's 10 or 11 or 42?
Does anyone ever stop and ask him what he really
wants to do?
Whose attention deficit is this?
No one is calling this child abused
It's 100 per cent doctor approved.

Alice Pero

MY FATHER'S FRIEND, MR. HARDY   *SIX POETS CONVERSE*

The birdhouse lies on its side
in young white snow
in Mr. Hardy's yard

The perch, broken off, protrudes
from a bulging drift — a dismembered finger
beckons little swallows

From my bedroom window
I detect dried twigs poking
from the dark hole — nest remnants

under a protective roof —
evidence of past habitation
I wonder why my father

let Mr. Hardy have it?
I remember handing dad the nails
my eyes squeezing shut

every time the hammer slammed
into the white pine, the way his fist
gripped the handle

round indentations appeared
on the smooth skin of the wood
like large thumb prints

My father didn't seem to notice
I didn't mention it
My father is dead

as well as Mr. Hardy
but the bird house survives
It hangs from a branch

over the fence
I see the nails have begun to pop
Dad should have used screws

   Mary Hazen-Stearns

BEYOND BABI YAR   *SIX POETS CONVERSE*

The blanched bones began to rise like leaves in an autumn wind
Some floated in space while others walked the ground
They danced before me to the sad song of memory
A sharp finger pointed to the dark abysmal pit filled with babies' shoes
golden rings and tattered rags next to fragile translucent skin
the skin already making shades to block out the light
I listened for their cries but only heard laughter's
crescendo under full moon's light
Is this the promised resurrection of the dead? And where is G-d?
The bones fell back quietly to their amaranthine bed
Tears like rain fell from the silver-studded sky
I saw a glow from a single match in the black hole below
I then knew the light had always been present
and I too laughed while whispering the familiar strains of Kaddish

   Ryfkah

PULLING A THREAD   *SIX POETS CONVERSE*

Luis lost everything:
his respect, his honour, his manhood.
Dignity died with loving attention
at his callous hands: a self-inflicted dearth
of reasoning as sure as suicide.

This is not an easy thing to accomplish.
But he was victorious:
He destroyed his life
and mangled many others.

I won't speak of the shame
that kept his wife hidden for years,
the tears of his children,
the bruises of the screaming night
that held them all breathless.

A home became a prison
and its warden its torturer.
This alone is enough
to make God weep —
but be warned, there are tears
of sadness and tears of anger.
Luis, do you know which bitter rain
is falling in your name?

No, the most pathetic aspect of Luis
is too well known in the whispers
of red-faced, black-eyed tyranny
echoing forever through the alleys
of our secret little houses
with their lamb-blooded doors.

Be careful upon which door you knock,
Luis. Lazy temptation makes us
break every taboo given time.
And time is all we have
when knocking out the portals of choice:
Even the blood of the lamb bites
the knuckles of the fist which raps
upon the hardwood splinters
of hatred and misunderstanding.
Knock too loud and the answer will arrive
behind you, an angel of fire
redeeming a message you forgot
in the angry streets while loving
families cower inside, beyond the portal
protected by prayers of understanding, solidarity
of will and action called compassion.

I want to speak of the worst
side of the fist: the irreparable harm
it does to a person, a family, a culture.
You see Luis did not beat an individual.
He outright trampled
a culture into the dust, and then spat on it.
His mucous: the venom of shame
in a mold-dry tomb of a mouth.

You would kiss your mother
with that maggot-infested grave, Luis?
"I do," it cackled at your wife
and that tongue flicked, serpent-like, at your children,
licking their eyes like grapes
while you dreamed of the wine
you could bottle if only you could trample
their heads and squeeze out the right vintage.

An old, sour vintage of pain
so foul it guts the innocent
can be passed down generation to generation
and yet still intoxicate the stupid
before spilling out again
to do its true damage.

There once were saints and knights
crusading across Aragon
and waving their long-sword honour above
their stallion-reared pride for all the world to see,
as unbending as Castile steel.

There once were explorers
unafraid of themselves reaching
the edges of the world, willing
to sail right off the maps
into the wet sphere of the unknown
and not only bring it back,
but colonize it, settle it, and love it.

There once were monks
who crossed the ocean
and crossed the found children
to teach them of love and charity —
though, it must be admitted, some fell down
upon meeting the same eternal fist
Luis also discovered. Hatred
crawls into people like demonic possession.

But stories and histories repeat
themselves like their madmen heirs.
However, a little awareness or a good library
as comfortable as the home of heritage
can make an exorcism of loss.

There once were tongues
babbling across the world
which turned quietly to mouth
the new vowels of the Iberian main
and teach and preach and reach
the mind, the heart, the soul.
It was a universal language
for a universal people: heart.

A knight, a captain, a father
cowled or uncowled, it is irrelevant:
they all tried to better the ground
upon which they stood, plow
the arid soil fallow, beget
a better tomorrow, uplift
the next generation with praise,
the open hands of a kiss, hugging
the future to the bosom of the past.

Sí, you see,
there is wisdom in yesterday
as only father and mother can teach.
Yet there is also retreat
from the light, ignorance
of the heart, lack

of compassion, hate
of self, loathing
of others which translates universally
into an unravelling of skeins
and a destruction of tapestries
it took eternal generations to weave.
There is one vast loom
with an infinity of weavers
weaving rainbows of people.

Just think of the consequences,
Luis, before you act. It takes only one hand
to pull a thread out of the world
and unravel us all.

Thomas Fortenberry

SARAH JANE PASSED THROUGH   *SIX POETS CONVERSE*

When Sarah Jane was three,
she saw a camel in a cloud and a horse in a rock;
and when she told her mother, Mommy said
"Don't be silly. Rocks are rocks and clouds are clouds."
(and thinking of Emily, went back to feeding Baby Alice.)
When Sarah Jane was five,
she went to kindergarten dressed in her sister Dora's dress
which had been preworn by her sister Clara
and Bobby Mills pinched her and made her cry,
calling her white trash and saying she smelled.
(Only Sarah's socks and underwear were new.)
When Sarah Jane was nine,
Bobby offered her a quarter
to go under the bleachers and lift her dress;
when she said no, he told Tommy she wanted a dollar;
and when she told her mommy,
her daddy belted her for leading the boys on
(and saying he was sorry, comforted her later that night.)
when Sarah Jane was fourteen,

Bobby asked her to the homecoming dance;
but her mother said she was too young
and her sisters wouldn't let her wear their old dresses.
instead Bobby took Mary Ann Witherspoon
from over at the trailer park.
(while Sarah Jane sat on her bed
and wrote in her special book.)
when Sarah Jane was eighteen,
she married Bobby Mills
and they moved in with his stepmother,
next to Mary Ann's parents in the trailer park
(and her momma cried for her baby Alice
and for losing Emily.
when Sarah Jane was nearly twenty
and expecting Little Donna's sister
they buried her in a cardboard casket
Bobby smashed her head for asking him
why he was out all night with Mary Ann Nelson
(and Alice's mother buried the special book with her)
When Donna was three years old

Gary Blankenship

HONEYSUCKLE NOISE *SIX POETS CONVERSE*

Brass chords toll, percussion rings
More than hurled words branded
and seared by the savage messiah —
her father dressed in olive drab

His watercolours exude spring
She breathes in creamy gardenias
Skirt brushes wisteria spills
rustles and sways along garden path

Against the rage of broken bottles
and whisky sours, she cowers in a corner
tethered down by fear. Violet blooms
in white flesh are carefully concealed

Fireworks burst from cups of blossoms
Lemon verbena scrambles toward sun
Intrigued how light affects colours
she rubs a petal across her cheek

His scenes are collected around the world. Painted
warmth glows inside cottage windows. His nature
masked behind pastel strokes, robust hues fed
by sweet peas and a daughter bent to his will

Ebb of beating wings and buzz
Squirrels scurry beneath a grape arbour
In melanite shadows across drowsy dusk
she knows a different serenity, listens
to hyacinth blue

Marylin Injeyan

BATTERED

Words rain down upon a battered heart
too weak to take a stand
too tired to voice an opinion
and much too fragile to walk away.

She holds onto the dream of peace
like a chalice deliberating her future
coffee stains taking the place
of the warm hands she craves.

She holds onto her thoughts
with a thread of unspoken conviction
as his terror demands she listen
but she can't hear him any more
her ears are deaf for her protection
her heart is wrapped safely
behind a wall that even he can't climb
Though he placed it there,
brick by brick.

starshine

A GOOD WOMAN

A good woman does what he says.
A good woman does what he wants.
A good woman accepts all of his criticism.
A good woman doesn't talk back.
A good woman accepts his punches.
A good woman hides the bruises.
A good woman is a good victim.

Silenced victims covered in shame
dare not speak
devastate a family name
instead bearing the burden than to bring porn to fame.
For who would believe
she must have liked it
they say.
I didn't hear her scream.
Neither did I.
Her body bears no scars, it must be a lie.
Like empty raindrops that fall and evaporate
so is the judicial magistrate.
While he is out in eight
she embraces a life sentence of hate ...

Susan Stone Salas

THE WOMEN

Out of the mist comes a hand
holding a hand holding a hand,
a long chain — mother, daughter,
the women march by, they are
one of the elements, ancient
as the earth and they call to her,
put the sacrificial knife in her hand.

She's courageous and brave.
The knife is lifted high,
comes down with a sigh,
cuts off lips and clitoris,
an offering to the reigning Phallus.

Deaf and blind,
he condescends to
accept the sacrifice
as a matter of convenience,
unaware of the
abyss
gaping
growing

Tammara Hayimi Slilat

PICNIC

It is all very strange
I just woke up and feel confused
Forest   birdsong   grass
those I recognize
This must be a picnic
yet where are the children?
I am sure they are fine
they are always fine
they must be.
I must have been sitting in a bad position
as I cannot feel my feet.
Sometimes you hurt me
why do you hurt me?
How nice!
My children they are here too
sleeping in the grassy shade.
Did you put them there?
They are very quiet
never this quiet.
The sun is warm and you have a shovel.
Do you love me?

Teemu Lahteenmaki

UNTITLED

Take this grief and weave it in song
Turn it to anger to upheave the wrongs
Undo this cycle, undo this pain
Pray for these families again and again!
Pray till their hearts can rise out of the flames
Pray till the world knows all their daughters' names
Sing out in prayer, pray out in song
Enough is enough: it's murder, it's WRONG.

TLC Birdsill

COTIDIANAS DE MI CIUDAD

Sola, inocente ... la noche
Miedo, frío ... llanto
Gritos, golpes ... sangre
Mujer, verdugos ... infamia
Inquietud, desconcierto, presentimientos, búsqueda,
Pesquisas, retratos, esperanza, tristeza ... realidad
Restos, funerales, familia, soledad, impotencia, coraje ... IMPUNIDAD

Valta Ortega

EL RÍO MURMURA EL DOLOR DE MARÍA

La ciudad amanece vestida de estragos
bebiendo mentiras.
El sol se apagó en marzo
y cayó en el orificio de la noche
que cubría las casas de todas las mujeres.
Las lágrimas de la luna tocaron a esta tierra
y la convirtieron en un mar de espanto.
La luna ya no canta en Ciudad Juárez
ayer se vistió de negro amargo
el río murmura el dolor de María
mientras el desierto en dos se parte.
Los dioses inundan el río
que se convierte en un pozo cargado de cadáveres.

Verónica Leiton

SI TAN SÓLO ESCUCHARAS ...
(Octubre 25 del 2002)

Si tan sólo escucharas un instante y volvieras la mirada a este hogar desolado,
sabrías cuánta miseria ronda por doquier
y cuán hondo es el abismal silencio con el que se yergue
un monumento a la injusticia.
Si tan sólo escucharas un instante,
llegaría hasta ti el gemir de tantas madres
que no hacen más que morir cada día
ante la angustiante espera que taladra los huesos,
y el no saber dónde reposará su cabeza
la pequeña que hace tiempo, no duerme en casa ...
Si tan sólo escucharas un instante,
alzarías la voz, unida a la de otras tantas
que hacen de su garganta un estandarte
cuyo emblema se alza en fiera lucha,
reclamando cada día un poco de paz.
Si tan solo escucharas un instante,
percibirías en el murmullo de la noche
las voces de tantos que han sido amordazadas
con el silencio de una fosa común.
Sabrías que cada nuevo día es un desgarrador grito
de esta tierra cuyo suelo teñido en púrpura
se rehúsa a guardar en su seno,
la sangre inocente de uno más de sus hijos,
vencido brutalmente ante el brazo asesino
de sus propios hermanos.
Si tan sólo escucharas un instante,
saltarías de tu asiento acojinado
y dejarías el mullido lecho donde duermes.
Proclamarías a los cuatro vientos tu repudio
a la mezquindad que compra y vende vidas ajenas,
y te levantarías erguido sobre las anónimas tumbas
que se esconden tras los cimientos de edificios blanqueados
con paredes de mármol y ventanales de cristal,
donde se archivan sueños y se regatean esperanzas.
Si tan sólo escucharas un instante,
descubrirías que entonces
y quizá sólo entonces,

podrías detener la violencia
por un momento ...

   Verónica Olivas

I LOVE YOU

crooked nose, which meets your fist
fierce palm to cheek, a cry suppressed,
my complaint i do repress —
how can i speak?
my tongue tied in a knot of fear
the smell of sweat, cigars and beer
i dream i'm any place but here
another life …
but why should ever i complain?
i have a roof to stop the rain
and never have i hunger pangs
to make me weak
the only thing i have to do
is cook and clean and care for you,
just like i always wanted to —
a perfect wife
and just be careful what i say
and not to stumble in your way
or drop the china dinner tray
or breathe too loud
and not to speak or sound too brave
or mention when you didn't shave
or when you told me to behave
with two black eyes;
i sat that night and wondered when
your violent reign would ever end
and, for a moment, if all men
were so allowed
if modern slave and wife were one
or if the bind could be undone
or, if i could, i'd ever run,
your love despise
i almost then decided to,
to run, to shout "so long!" to you,
to let the bruises, black and blue,
fade eternally
but, a thought came creeping in —
this battle i will never win

you'll only have me back again;
you always do
so ... here i sit, and here i stay,
day and night, night and day,
rehearsing words i'll never say:
"today i'm leaving"
and now i lay inside a box
under dirt and grass and rocks
and the stone above me quietly mocks
"I loved you"

Windy Sue

THE PROMISES

On this white day under our Lord's presence I give you my promises.
I promise to love you through all tribulations. If you love me too.
Don't obsess over me
I promise to be your best friend if you are mine. Don't turn away from me
I promise to be the mother of your children. If you are the father.
Don't abandon them I promise not to cry. If you don't beat me.
Please don't hurt me.
I promise not to complain. If you respect me.
Please don't humiliate me.
I promise dinner ready by eight. If you have patience.
Please don't scream at me.
I promise you pleasure in our bed. If you give me love.
Please don't force yourself upon me.
I promise to give you my life. If you don't take it away.
Please let me live.
With these promises, my love, I give myself to you.

    Yéssica

A Selection of Our Titles in Print

A Fredericton Alphabet (John Leroux) photos, architecture, ISBN 1-896647-77-4
All the Perfect Disguises (Lorri Neilsen Glenn) poetry, 1-55391-010-9
Antimatter (Hugh Hazelton) poetry, 1-896647-98-7
Avoidance Tactics (Sky Gilbert) drama, 1-896647-50-2
Bathory (Moynan King) drama, 1-896647-36-7
Break the Silence (Denise DeMoura) poetry, 1-896647-87-1
Combustible Light (Matt Santateresa) poetry, 0-921411-97-9
Crossroads Cant (Mary Elizabeth Grace, Mark Seabrook, Shafiq, Ann Shin. Joe Blades, editor) poetry, 0-921411-48-0
Cuerpo amado/ Beloved Body (Nela Rio; Hugh Hazelton, translator) poetry, 1-896647-81-2
Dark Seasons (Georg Trakl; Robin Skelton, translator) poetry, 0-921411-22-7
Day of the Dog-tooth Violets (Christina Kilbourne) fiction, 1-896647-44-8
During Nights That Undress Other Nights/ En las noches que desvisten otras noches (Nela Rio; Elizabeth Gamble Miller, translator) poetry, 1-55391-008-7
for a cappuccino on Bloor (kath macLean) poetry, 0-921411-74-X
Great Lakes logia (Joe Blades, editor) art & writing anthology, 1-896647-70-7
Heart-Beat of Healing (Denise DeMoura) poetry, 0-921411-24-3
Heaven of Small Moments (Allan Cooper) poetry, 0-921411-79-0
Herbarium of Souls (Vladimir Tasic) short fiction, 0-921411-72-3
I Hope It Don't Rain Tonight (Phillip Igloliorti) poetry, 0-921411-57-X
I Love You: 65 international poets united against violence against women (Gino d'Artali, ed.) poetry, 0-921411-31-6
Jive Talk: George Fetherling in Interviews and Documents (Joe Blades, editor), 1-896647-54-5
Mangoes on the Maple Tree (Uma Parameswaran) fiction, 1-896647-79-0
Manitoba highway map (rob mclennan) poetry, 0-921411-89-8
Paper Hotel (rob mclennan) poetry, 1-55391-004-4
Railway Station (karl wendt) poetry, 0-921411-82-0
Reader Be Thou Also Ready (Robert James) fiction, 1-896647-26-X
resume drowning (Jon Paul Fiorentino) poetry, 1-896647-94-4
Rum River (Raymond Fraser) fiction, 0-921411-61-8
Shadowy:Technicians: New Ottawa Poets (rob mclennan, editor), poetry, 0-921411-71-5
Singapore (John Palmer) drama, 1-896647-85-5
Song of the Vulgar Starling (Eric Miller) poetry, 0-921411-93-6
Speaking Through Jagged Rock (Connie Fife) poetry, 0-921411-99-5
Starting from Promise (Lorne Dufour) poetry, 1-896647-52-9
Sunset (Pablo Urbanyi; Hugh Hazelton, translator) fiction, 1-55391-014-1
Sweet Mother Prophesy (Andrew Titus) fiction, 1-55391-002-8
Tales for an Urban Sky (Alice Major) poetry, 1-896647-11-1
The Longest Winter (Julie Doiron, Ian Roy) photos, short fiction, 0-921411-95-2
This Day Full of Promise (Michael Dennis) poetry, 1-896647-48-0
The Sweet Smell of Mother's Milk-Wet Bodice (Uma Parameswaran) fiction, 1-896647-72-3
The Yoko Ono Project (Jean Yoon) drama, 1-55391-001-X
Túnel de proa verde/ Tunnel of the Green Prow (Nela Rio; Hugh Hazelton, translator) poetry, 0-921411-80-4
What Was Always Hers (Uma Parameswaran) short fiction, 1-896647-12-X

www.brokenjaw.com hosts our current catalogue, submissions guidelines, manuscript award competitions, booktrade sales representation and distribution information. Broken Jaw Press eBooks of selected titles are available from http://www.PublishingOnline.com. Directly from us, all individual orders must be prepaid. All Canadian orders must add 7% GST/HST (CCRA Business Number: 892667403NP0001).

BROKEN JAW PRESS Inc., Box 596 Stn A, Fredericton NB E3B 5A6, Canada